Scissor-Tales for Special Days

Storytelling Cutups, Activities & Extensions

Written & Illustrated
by
Jan Grubb Philpot

SARAH'S PRIZE EGG

WHO'S THAT RAPPING?

THE PILGRIMS FIND A GOBLIN

Rain, Dear?

Incentive Publications, Inc.
Nashville, Tennessee

Illustrated by Jan Grubb Philpot
Cover by Jan Grubb Philpot
Edited by Jan Keeling

ISBN 0-86530-284-7

PRINTED IN THE UNITED STATES OF AMERICA

TABLE OF CONTENTS

SCISSOR-TALE STORYTELLING FOR SPECIAL DAYS

Preface

The idea of providing fascinating visual reinforcement while telling a story is not a new one. Nor is the idea of telling a story while cutting out paper "pictures." *Scissor-Tales for Special Days* (and its companion *Scissor-Tales for Any Day*) is a unique collection of brand-new stories and poems to share at special times throughout the year. Each story comes complete with patterns, step-by-step instructions, and (best of all!) at least one meaningful classroom extension. Although this book was primarily intended to "add spice" to the classroom or library, it is, in reality, a book every library should have two of—one for kids and one for their adult friends! This book is for everyone!

Little ones will be enthralled with the short stories incorporating all of those elements little ones love: rhyme and rhythm, make-believe, and surprise. Their eyes will light up in wonder as they watch the paper "magic" appear.

Older Kids will enjoy mastering the paper "magic" to share with young friends. They will love being one of the "Paper Caper People" (see page 67) and visiting primary classrooms to perform their craft.

Teachers will find "paper caper storytelling" a unique way to introduce concepts or simply to add spice to the school day. They will be pleased to note that each story is easily integrated with basic skills or with a learning experience, and that activity suggestions follow each story.

Parents, too, can have fun sharing these stories when serving as parent volunteers in the school, in scout meetings, in church groups, and when spending time with their own children!

Happy Times Ahead!

SCISSOR - TALES STORYTELLING TIPS

Although none of the paper capers in this book are complicated, you will find that some are quite simple and others call for some practice before telling. You will also find that some are "one time" paper capers and that others can be used again and again! All of the stories come with complete instructions; however, reading the following tips will reinforce these instructions and provide some extra hints for success.

SCISSOR-TALE LINGO

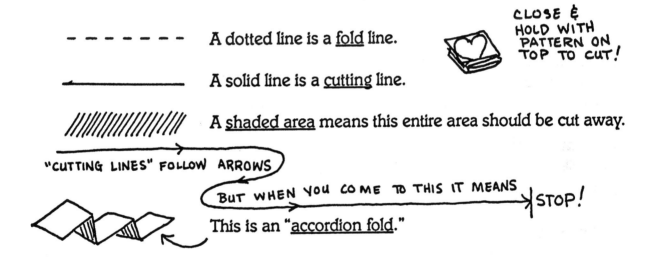

– – – – – – – – A dotted line is a <u>fold</u> line.

——————→ A solid line is a <u>cutting</u> line.

///////////// A <u>shaded area</u> means this entire area should be cut away.

"CUTTING LINES" FOLLOW ARROWS

BUT WHEN YOU COME TO THIS IT MEANS → STOP!

This is an "<u>accordion fold</u>."

CLOSE & HOLD WITH PATTERN ON TOP TO CUT!

OTHER TIPS

Some stories like "Rain, Dear?" and "Josh's Welcome Home" can be made once and used over again many times. To ensure long-lasting usage, laminate!

These same two stories require the cutting out of certain areas inside paper boundaries. A utility knife (the kind with a narrow slanted blade) does a perfect job.

A few of the stories require that two pages or pieces be glued together prior to telling. The best way to do this without making bubbles or runny glue is to use rubber cement. Spread rubber cement on the back of each piece and allow to dry. After both pieces are dry, put them together—you will have an instant smooth bond.

Sometimes a pattern calls for duplication on black paper. Simply reproduce on regular paper, cut out, and trace around the edges with chalk onto the black paper.

TELLING THE STORIES

Of course, you can tell the stories exactly as they are written, but feel free to tell them in your own words. It is the nature of storytelling that each performer adds his or her unique touch to the telling of a tale. Knowing that you may tell the story in your own words can calm you, prevent you from worrying about telling the story wrong, and make your entire presentation seem much more natural.

If you don't feel comfortable telling the story as you do a scissor-tale, record the story (pausing at appropriate moments) and play the tape as you present the story. Or, you may learn the story well enough to simply glance down at a written copy as you speak. Another idea is to give several students copies of the verse and let them read as you cut.

There are many ways to share the poems and stories in the book, and it is fine to choose any method with which you feel comfortable. Just enjoy!

A HALLOWEEN SCISSOR-TALE

PREPARATION: Duplicate page 11 on yellow paper. Cut out shaded areas at bottom of paper. Your paper should look like this:

Fold up tail as shown. Now fold paper lengthwise on the fold line as shown. Be sure cutting line pattern is on the out-side toward you.

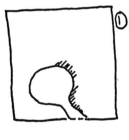

FOLD "TAIL" UP ON BLANK SIDE OF PAPER.

NOW FOLD PAPER IN HALF WITH "TAIL" INSIDE AND PATTERN ON OUTSIDE.

WHO'S THAT RAPPING?

Once there was a witch. She was a very lonely witch. "If only I had a cat," she thought. "Not a black cat like every other witch in town, but a big, yellow cat to keep me company. Then I wouldn't be so lonely." However, the witch did not have a yellow cat, so she sat down with a book to read for a spell.

(Hold paper out in front of you as if you are reading a book of "spells." Be careful to keep back side with cat pattern hidden behind your hand.)

Before long, the lonely old witch heard something: a soft rap, a gentle tap, a quiet knock upon her door. The old witch looked up and said, "Who's that rapping? Who's that tapping? Who's that knocking on my door?" There was no answer, so the witch began again to read for a spell. Then it came once more: a soft rap, a gentle tap, a quiet knock upon the door. "Who's that rapping? Who's that tapping? Who's that knocking on my door?" called the old witch, a little louder this time. No answer! "Well, enough of this!" cried the witch, and she rose from her chair and went to the door. She peered out into the inky black night, but all she saw was a big yellow moon.

(Fold down uncut "cat's tail." Then close "book," leaving "moon" hanging out.)

She looked behind the door *(cut on line 1 and stop)*. Nothing there. She walked around the front of the house *(cut line 2)* and around the side of the house *(cut line 3)*. Still, she saw nothing. She walked around the back of her house *(cut line 4)*. Nothing there either. She came back to the front of her house and walked all the way down her front walk *(cut line 5)*. Not a thing did she see!

The old witch trotted right back up her front walk and into her house. "Maybe the soft rap, the gentle tap, the quiet knock came from inside my house," she muttered. And so she looked *(cut on line 6 as you speak)* around and around and around her house. Not a thing did she find, but suddenly came the soft rap, the gentle tap, the quiet knock, and this time she knew it came from her door.

"This is quite enough!" stated the old witch, and she cried out very loudly, "Who's that rapping? Who's that tapping? Who's that knocking on my door?" No answer! The witch jumped up, marched to the door, jerked it open . . . and there sat a big yellow cat!

(open up cat)

CUTTING LINE 5

CUTTING LINE 4

CUTTING LINE 3

CUTTING LINE 2

CUTTING LINE 1

FOLD LINE

FOLD LINE

SPELLS

① IN PREPARATION, CUT OUT SHADED AREAS

CUTTING LINE 6

EXTENDING THE STORY

WHO'S THAT RAPPING?

Extend "Who's That Rapping?" with another story about witches that is also a lesson in following instructions. Have students take out a piece of paper and a pencil, and follow the same steps you make as you tell this story and draw it on the blackboard.

(Note: You do not draw everything over again each time. Simply add new portions of the drawing.)

① Witches have two pointy hats — one for everyday and one for special days.

② They have two speedy brooms to fly on — one for everyday and one for special days.

③ On nights of
     BIG
        FULL
           MOONS...

12

④ Witches cook up a magic
bubbling brew in their
very best magic pot,

⑤ Call their trusty pet
      BAT,

⑥ And fly through the air
      THIS   WAY

⑦   And   THAT
      Astride a broom
      With a big black
            CAT!

(Point to the cat.)

13

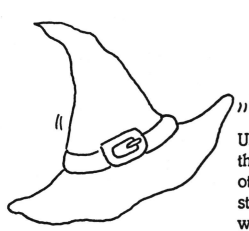

Extending the story into writing

Use this story as an opportunity to call attention to an area that will increase students' writing skills. Ask students what other words were used for the action word "knock" in the story. "Rap" and "tap," of course! And what other words were used to describe the "rap," the "tap," and the "knock"? "A *soft* rap, a *gentle* tap, a *quiet* knock." Explain that sometimes words are overused, and then they get old and tired. They lose their flavor and no longer do listeners (who have heard these same words once too often) feel the magic and appeal they might feel if a different word were used. Brainstorm with students for a list of tired and overused words frequently used in writing assignments.

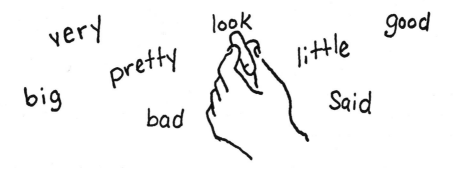

Assign each word to a group of students. Have them head a sheet of paper with the word and then work together to create a list of alternatives that they could use when they are writing. Bind all of the lists (including some blank pages for "tired" words that occur to students later) into a book and title it "In Other Words." Keep the book on the students' resource shelf or in your writing and publishing center. When students are revising their writing efforts they can consult it for "other words" to replace the "tired" ones! They might also add to the book "other words" they think of along the way.

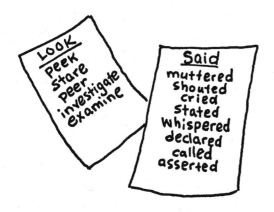

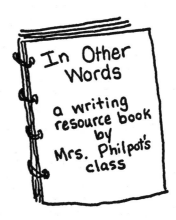

JOSH'S WELCOME HOME

A HALLOWEEN SCISSOR-TALE

PREPARATION: Here's a story that will keep goosebumps rising until the very end! Although a bit of preparation is required, all of the patterns are simple, and all but one can be used to tell the story again and again. You will need colored paper, one sheet of each of the following colors: yellow, red, white, green, and black. You will also need one sheet of paper that is orange on one side and black on the other (you can make this by gluing a sheet of orange paper to a sheet of black paper or by coloring one side of a sheet of orange construction paper black). The yellow paper has no pattern; it remains blank. The patterns for the other colors are found on the following pages: black/orange, page 19; red, page 20; white, page 21; green, page 22; black, page 23. Duplicate patterns on the appropriately colored sheets and cut out where indicated.

READY TO TELL THE STORY: In front of you, stack the patterns in the following order (top to bottom): red on top, then white, green, and, last of all, black. Separately, lay your black/orange paper over the top of your yellow paper so that black is on top and a yellow face gleams through the cutouts. Now, let's go a-haunting!

JOSH'S WELCOME HOME

Josh hurried home through the dark moonless night. Usually his paper route didn't take too long, but this evening the papers had arrived late, and old Mrs. Perkins had taken ages to find just the right change for him. Then, too, the days were getting shorter, and, early in the afternoon, the darkness began to fall steadily like a black velvet stage curtain. Josh's feet moved quickly over the crackling leaves, and he imagined they were old bone chips rattling beneath him. Josh had a good imagination, especially at Halloween— and when he was alone in the dark. He didn't like to admit he was nervous, but he was.

Josh peered into the inky blackness and through the looming tree shapes, trying to catch a glimpse of the porch light that would signal home was near. That was when he saw it—and he stopped dead in his tracks, his blood throbbing in his temples like the fast beat of a voodoo drum. He closed his eyes, willing away what he saw, but when he opened them, it was still there—the eyes burning fiercer than ever.

(Hold up your black "face" with the yellow paper behind it.)

Josh stood very still for a long time, his hair prickling on the top of his scalp, but the thing came no closer. "I know I am going the right way," he thought, "but I'll go a little off the path and maybe this thing won't follow me." And so he did, but when he looked up again, the thing was still watching him through the trees.

"What can it be?" he thought, "and what will I see when I get closer?" His heart pounded, and his knees quivered. When he looked again, he thought he saw two red eyes glittering in the center of those fierce yellow slits!

(Overlay your "face" with the red pattern.)

"This only happens in movies," he thought. "It only happens on TV, in books—it can't be happening to me!" Josh edged around another tree, trying hard to stay near the path that led home. He ventured another glance and thought he saw two gleaming white tusks over that jagged hungry mouth.

(Overlay your red pattern with the white pattern.)

"No!" he thought. "If this is what the thing's face looks like, what must the rest of it be? I'll bet it has feet with long pointy nails!"

(Overlay white pattern with green pattern.)

"And it must have arms about a hundred feet long with claws so sharp they can. . . I wonder what it eats?"

(Overlay green pattern with black pattern.)

Josh's knees turned to jelly. He leaned against the nearest tree and slid to the ground. "This is crazy," he said. "It can't be happening, so it must be my imagination. Everyone says I have a wild imagination. It has to be my imagination!" So, putting every ounce of determination to work, Josh willed away the arms with claws.

(Remove black pattern.)

He thought still harder, and the ugly feet with pointy nails were no longer there.

(Remove green pattern.)

He willed away the gleaming white tusks *(remove white pattern)*, and he willed away the glittering red eyes.

(Remove red pattern.)

But try as he would, he could not make the fierce burning face go away. "Home is that way," he thought, "and that's the way I'm going. I just won't think about it, and maybe it won't be there."

(Fold up "face" with yellow paper inside, as shown.)

So, carefully avoiding the sight of the hungry, fierce face and keeping his eyes on the ground as much as possible, Josh headed home.

He went around a tree,   *(cut as shown)*

and up a path,   *(cut as shown)*

around another tree,   *(cut as shown)*

and up the walk to his very own house.

(Cut as shown.)

He finally looked up as he heard his sister squeal, "Josh, you're home! How do you like my jack-o-lantern?"

(Slide yellow paper behind and open up to reveal the "fierce face" that has been haunting Josh.)

orange
side
out
with yellow
paper
behind

Reproduce on black paper (see "Tips" in front of book).
Cut out. Cut out spaces for facial features.
Slip a blank sheet of yellow paper cut to the same size
behind.

← outside cutting line →

Reproduce on red paper & cut out. Cut out indicated inside areas.

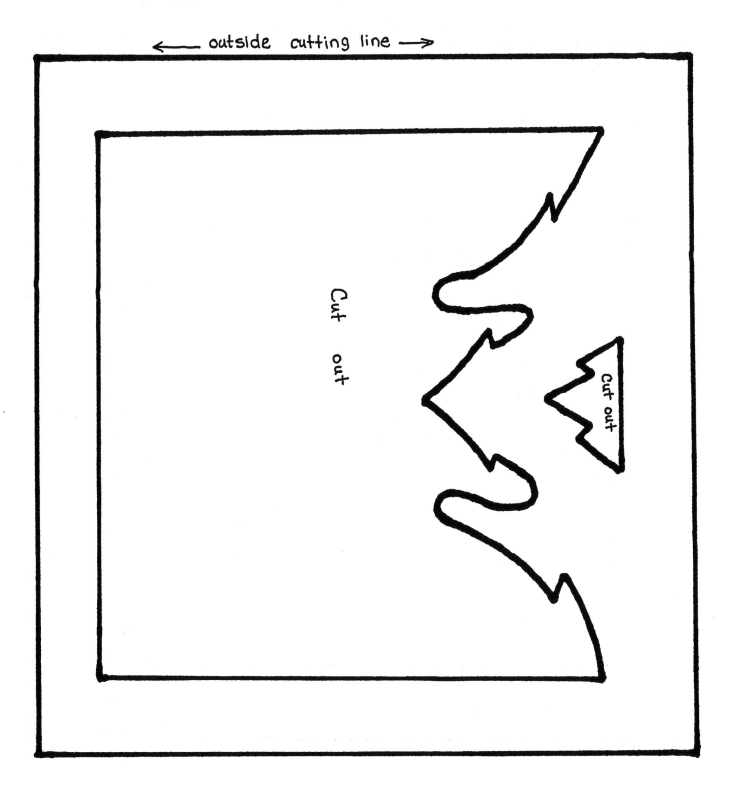

outside cutting line

Cut out

Cut out

Reproduce on white paper. Cut out along outside line. Cut out inside area.

← outside cutting line →

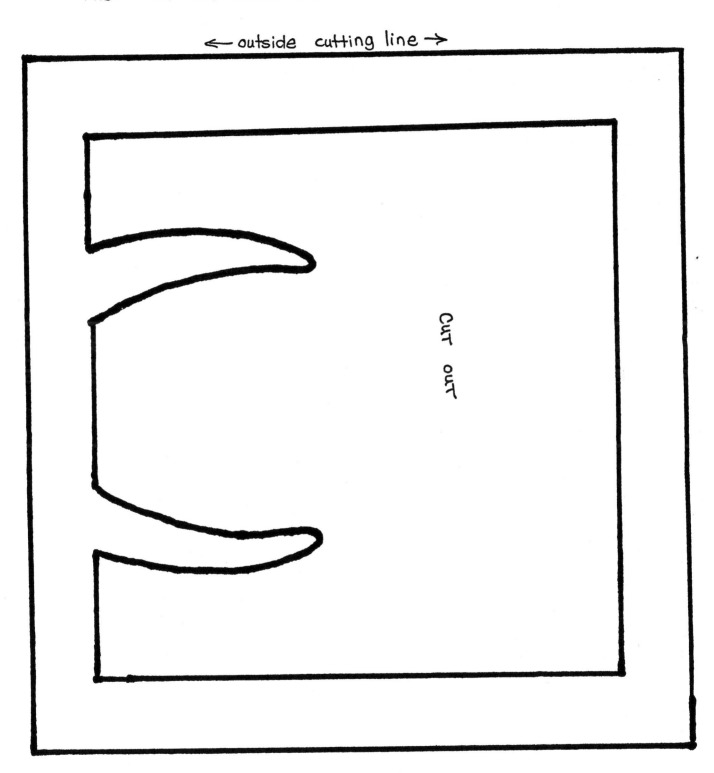

Cut out

Reproduce on green paper. Cut out on outside cutting line. Cut out inside area.

←— outside cutting line —→

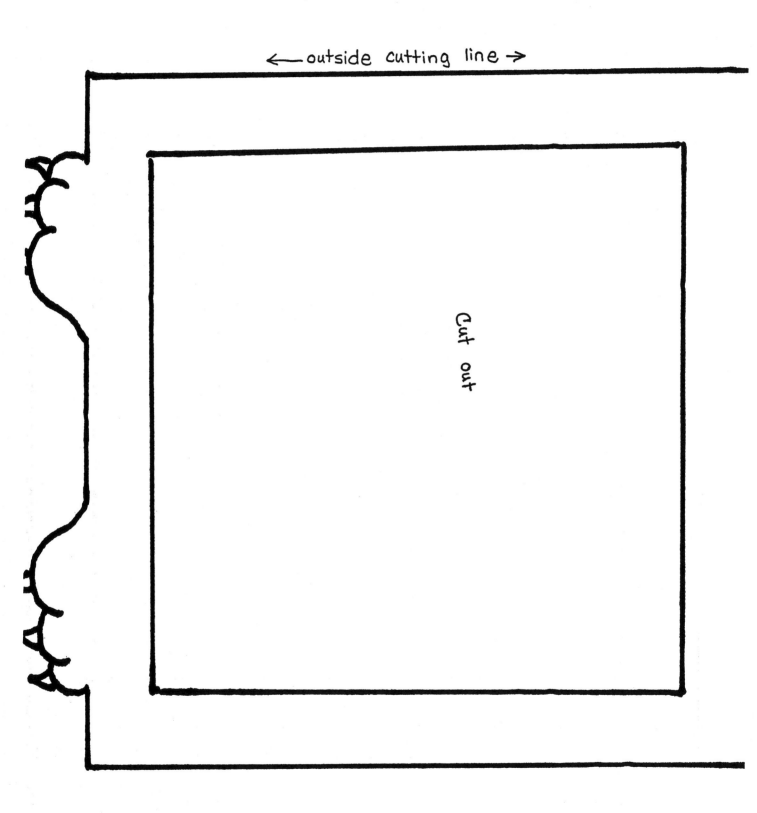

Cut out

← outside cutting line →

Cut out

Reproduce on black paper (see "Tips" in front of book). Cut out on outside cutting line. Cut out inside area.

Extending the story...
JOSH'S WELCOME HOME

Read to your class these popular children's books about real and imaginary fears:

The Ghost-Eye Tree by Bill Martin and John Achambault (Henry Holt & Co.)
Ghost's Hour, Spook's Hour by Eve Bunting (Cleary)

Discuss real and imaginary fears with your class. What are some fears that are totally unreasonable? What are some fears that are reasonable? In the story, Josh allowed his imagination to run away with an imaginary fear. All of us have imagined monsters at times. Maybe we thought we saw something out of the corner of our eye, maybe we heard a creak on the stairs, maybe something mysteriously moved from where we thought it was. Have students write about "The monster that turned out to be . . . " A good story with this theme is found on Jackie Torrence's storytelling record *Tales for Scary Times* (Earwig, 1985). The name of the story is "Tillie."

The scissor-tale in this story is fascinating to watch, and similar ones are fairly simple for students to reproduce if they remember to overlay one page with another and to trace the original before creating the next page. The concept is similar to the technique used in Lois Ehlert's *Color Farm* and *Color Zoo* (J.B. Lippincott). Share these picture books with students and challenge them to create their own cut-out picture stories. Some ideas follow.

• A man who changes colors (overlay with cellophane)

• A woman whose nose grows (each overlay features a larger nose)

• How to turn into a witch (pattern of a person—each overlay features a change in costume: dress changes to black, buckles are added to shoes, pointy black hat replaces flowered one, etc.)

• Changes a tree undergoes during the year

• Change from animal to animal, as in Lois Ehlert's stories

24

A Thanksgiving Scissor-Tale

PREPARATION: Duplicate the turkey head pattern on page 27. Use brown paper, or color pattern brown, and cut out. Duplicate the turkey body pattern on page 28. Do not cut out. Glue turkey head pattern on blank side of the body pattern three inches from the bottom of the page, as shown below.

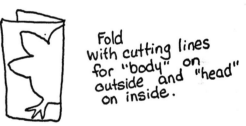

← glue in center ON BACK OF sheet "body" is reproduced on.

3"

Fold page in half lengthwise with cutting lines for turkey body pattern as shown below.

Fold with cutting lines for "body" on outside and "head" on inside.

THE PILGRIMS FIND A GOBLIN!

A long time ago when Pilgrims first came to America, two Pilgrim fathers were out chopping wood to keep their families warm during the long winter days ahead. Suddenly, their children came running from the forest. "Oh, Daddy!" they cried. "Come quickly! It's a goblin!"

"A goblin?" asked one father.

"There's no such thing as a goblin," stated the other father.

"Yes, there is!" cried the oldest boy.

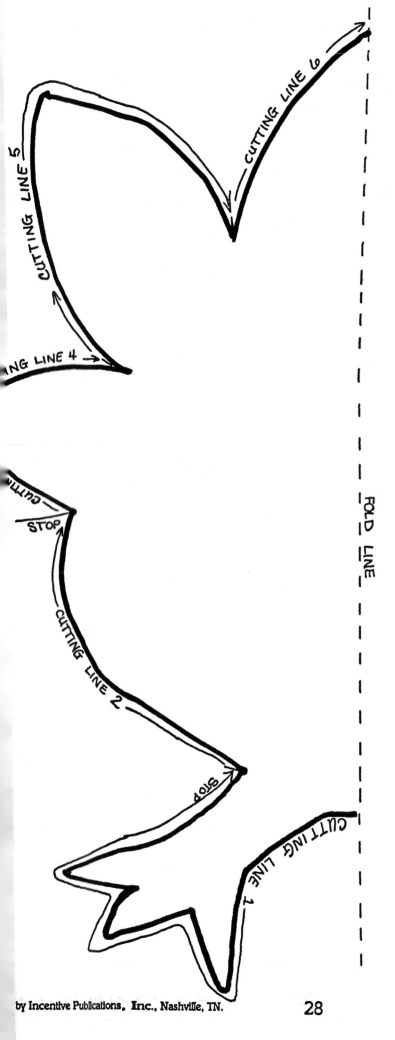

CUTTING LINE 6

CUTTING LINE 5

CUTTING LINE 4 →

CUTTING STOP

CUTTING LINE 2

CUTTING LINE 1

STOP

FOLD LINE

"And it has big pointy feet like THIS!" asserted the girl *(cut out feet)*.

"And it's big and fat like THIS!" shouted the youngest *(cut on line 2)*.

The children were so certain that they had seen a goblin that the fathers began to look for it. They searched this way *(cut on line 3)*, and they searched that way *(cut on line 4)*, around this tree *(cut on line 5)*, and around that tree *(cut on line 6)*.

Suddenly one of the children pointed and shouted, "There it is, and it's a goblin!" The fathers looked in the direction the girl had pointed. There stood a great big turkey—sure enough, "a goblin"!

(Open up turkey and turn around so that head shows.)

The Pilgrims find a Goblin!

A Thanksgiving Scissor-Tale

PREPARATION: Duplicate the turkey head pattern on page 27. Use brown paper, or color pattern brown, and cut out. Duplicate the turkey body pattern on page 28. Do not cut out. Glue turkey head pattern on blank side of the body pattern three inches from the bottom of the page, as shown below.

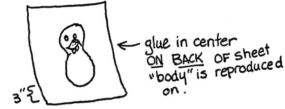

← glue in center
ON BACK OF sheet
"body" is reproduced
on.

3"

Fold page in half lengthwise with cutting lines for turkey body pattern as shown below.

Fold
with cutting lines
for "body" on
outside and "head"
on inside.

THE PILGRIMS FIND A GOBLIN!

A long time ago when Pilgrims first came to America, two Pilgrim fathers were out chopping wood to keep their families warm during the long winter days ahead. Suddenly, their children came running from the forest. "Oh, Daddy!" they cried. "Come quickly! It's a goblin!"

"A goblin?" asked one father.

"There's no such thing as a goblin," stated the other father.

"Yes, there is!" cried the oldest boy.

"And it has big pointy feet like THIS!" asserted the girl *(cut out feet)*.

"And it's big and fat like THIS!" shouted the youngest *(cut on line 2)*.

The children were so certain that they had seen a goblin that the fathers began to look for it. They searched this way *(cut on line 3)*, and they searched that way *(cut on line 4)*, around this tree *(cut on line 5)*, and around that tree *(cut on line 6)*.

Suddenly one of the children pointed and shouted, "There it is, and it's a goblin!" The fathers looked in the direction the girl had pointed. There stood a great big turkey—sure enough, "a goblin"!

(Open up turkey and turn around so that head shows.)

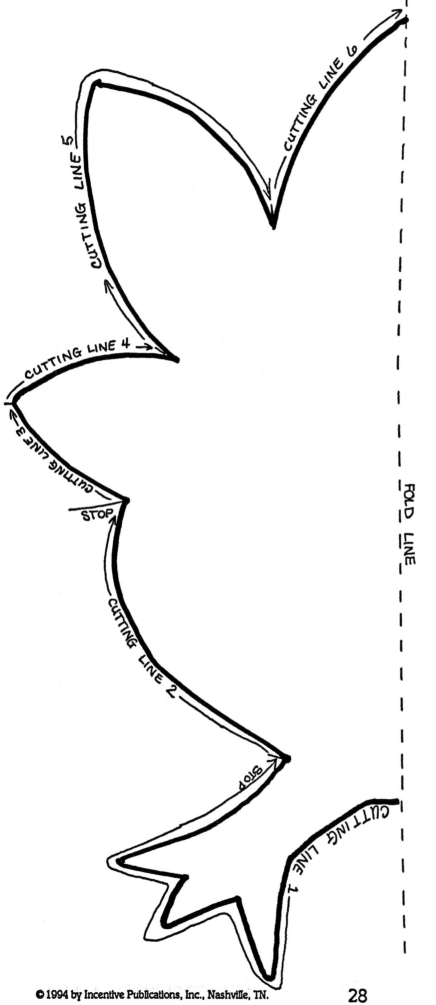

FOLD LINE

CUTTING LINE 6

CUTTING LINE 5

CUTTING LINE 4 →

CUTTING LINE 3

STOP

CUTTING LINE 2

STOP

CUTTING LINE 1

TRACKING DOWN ANIMALS

The Pilgrim fathers in the story tracked down a "goblin" and found out that it was nothing more frightening than a turkey. See if you can track down animals! Below are the tracks left by a deer, a rabbit, a fox, a squirrel, a bear, a duck, and a robin. Which track belongs to which animal? When you are finished, you can check yourself by looking at the key at the bottom of the page. Then find out more about the animal of your choice. On a separate piece of paper, draw a picture of it, its natural home, and its usual dinner.

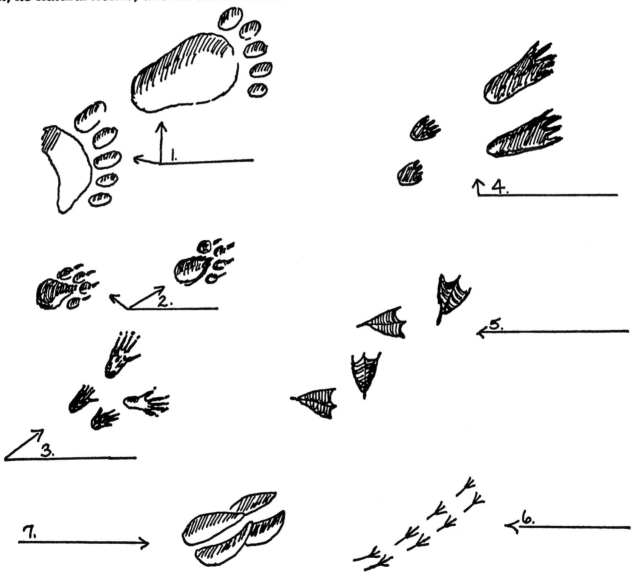

Name _____

Key: 1. Bear 2. Fox 3. Squirrel 4. Rabbit 5. Duck 6. Robin 7. Deer

RAIN, DEAR?

A Christmas Scissor-Tale

PREPARATION: Although this story requires a bit of preparation, this need be done only once to be able to tell the story many times. Duplicate pages 32 and 33. Color reindeer and other items appropriate colors. Cut out indicated white areas, making sure centers stay attached to borders, as shown. Make two copies of the door on page 34, cut out, and fold along indicated line. Glue reindeer page to page with umbrella and other items, gluing blank sides together. You will see that you have a picture on each side with cut-out spaces. All stays together because of the border. Attach a door to each side of the picture, as shown below.

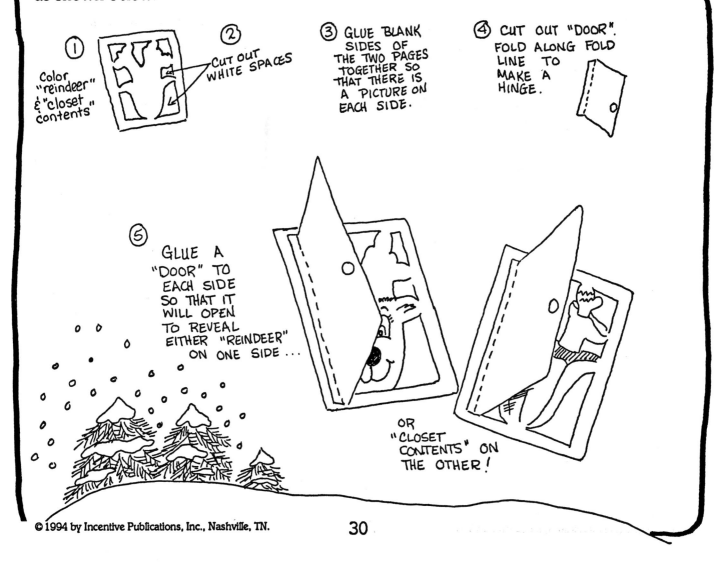

① Color "reindeer" & "closet contents"

② Cut out white spaces

③ GLUE BLANK SIDES OF THE TWO PAGES TOGETHER SO THAT THERE IS A PICTURE ON EACH SIDE.

④ CUT OUT "DOOR". FOLD ALONG FOLD LINE TO MAKE A HINGE.

⑤ GLUE A "DOOR" TO EACH SIDE SO THAT IT WILL OPEN TO REVEAL EITHER "REINDEER" ON ONE SIDE ...

OR "CLOSET CONTENTS" ON THE OTHER!

RAIN, DEAR?
A CHRISTMAS SCISSOR-TALE

One cold winter night, a little old man went to his door and looked outside. He turned to his wife and said, "Oh, look! It looks like reindeer!"

"Rain, dear? Oh my!" exclaimed the little old woman. She went to the closet and this is what she grabbed.

(Open closet door showing umbrella, etc.)

"Whatever is all that jumble?" asked the little old man.

"Well, granted it is a jumble," replied the little old woman, "but it's what you'll need for the rain, dear. There are your umbrella, your galoshes, and your mittens—you should stay quite dry in the rain, dear."

"My dear!" exclaimed the little old man. "Do leave all that jumble in the closet!"

"But don't you need it for the rain, dear?"

"My dear wife," replied the little old man, "you have quite forgotten what night this is!"

"No, I haven't" answered the little old woman. "It is Christmas Eve. But what has this to do with rain, dear?"

"Open the door and you will see, dear."

And so she did. *(Turn the closet around and open outside door.)* What she saw was the reindeer!

CUT OUT

CUT OUT WHITE SPACE

CUT OUT

CUT OUT

CUT OUT

GLUE "DOOR" HINGE HERE

CUT OUT WHITE SPACE

CUT OUT WHITE SPACE

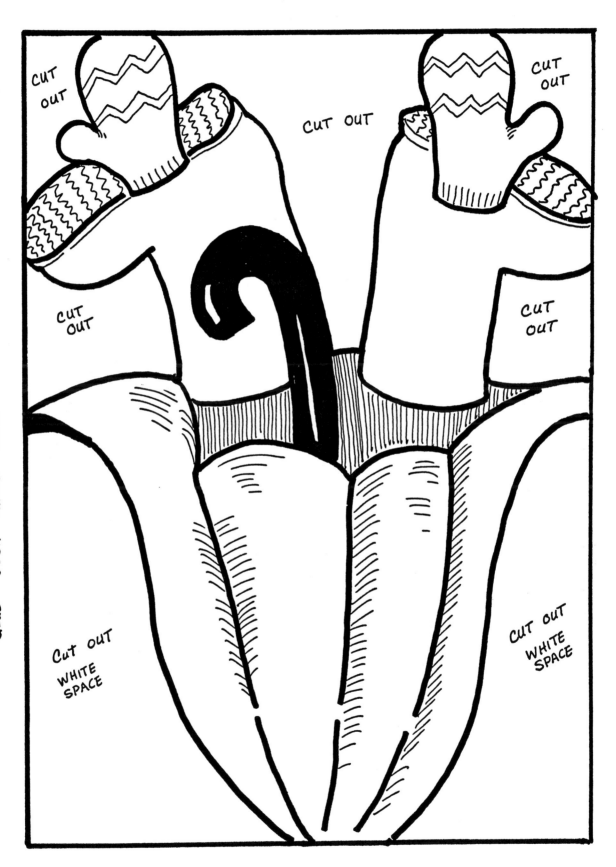

COLOR "DOOR" OR DUPLICATE ON COLORED PAPER.
CUT OUT.

MAKE <u>2</u> COPIES!

SPREAD GLUE ALONG EDGE & GLUE TO BORDERS.

FOLD LINE

RAIN, DEAR?

Homophones are words that are pronounced alike but differ in meaning, origin, or spelling. The little old man and the little old woman in the story misunderstood each other because of the homophones they used in their sentences. Homophone pairs, illustrated, can be cute and sometimes hilarious. Let each student make a list of homophones and illustrate a phrase using both words. You can use the homophone list below or the suggested phrases and sentences on the next page. Have students look up the meanings of any words they don't understand.

boar/bore	bread/bred
herd/heard	red/read
sail/sale	blue/blew
hair/hare	yew/you
aye/eye	side/sighed
hear/here	pair/pear
beau/bow	brake/break
sight/site	mail/male
cede/seed	son/sun
weigh/way	soar/sore
in/inn	meat/mete
dough/doe	carat/carrot
be/bee	to/two/too
waist/waste	dew/due
wear/ware	hay/hey
so/sew	hoes/hose
shoo/shoe	might/mite
right/write	cereal/serial
tale/tail	would/wood
hole/whole	tide/tied
core/corps	peek/peak

HOMOPHONES to ILLUSTRATE!

Illustrate these homophone phrases and sentences, or make your own.

I heard the herd.

A bored board

A sail sale

A hare with red hair

A beau with a bow

Which way to weigh?

Walk the wok.

Shoo away the shoe.

A tied tide

He blew until he was blue.

You in a yew

The scent of a cent

He read until he turned red.

The wood would!

Styling hair for a hare

A doe in the dough

The pear has a pair.

A mite with might

A hoes and hose store

A feet feat

A nose knows.

The tail end of a tale

Merry Mary gets married.

Sight the site.

A bare bear

A fair fare

Tow the toe.

May's maze

Pause for paws.

A clause about claws

A sole with soul

Our hour

Soar for a sore.

A coop for a coup

Bore the boar.

See the sea.

The flue flew.

The male gets mail.

Wait for weight.

The grate is great!

Flour the flower.

The road rode.

SHADOWS
a supplement for Groundhog Day

PREPARATION: The "paper caper" for this selection may be made once and used again and again. Reproduce page 38. Using a precision utility knife, cut around the figures on the heavy lines only. Do not cut on lighter solid lines or on dotted lines. The lighter solid lines remain attached to the paper, and the dotted lines are creased so that the figure folds outward. Put a black sheet of construction paper behind this sheet, gluing along edges only.

FOLD CUT EDGES TO RIGHT TO REVEAL "SHADOWS"

SHADOWS

Shadows are such funny things;
They're with you everywhere.
They like to do what you do;
Jump here, your shadow jumps there!
> *(Fold first figure outward to reveal shadow.)*

I never have to worry
About being alone, you see,
Because if I look behind,
My shadow is following me.
> *(Fold second figure outward to reveal shadow.)*

My shadow's such a copycat.
It must think I'm always right!
Whatever I do, wherever I go,
It keeps me always in sight.
> *(Fold third figure outward to reveal shadow.)*

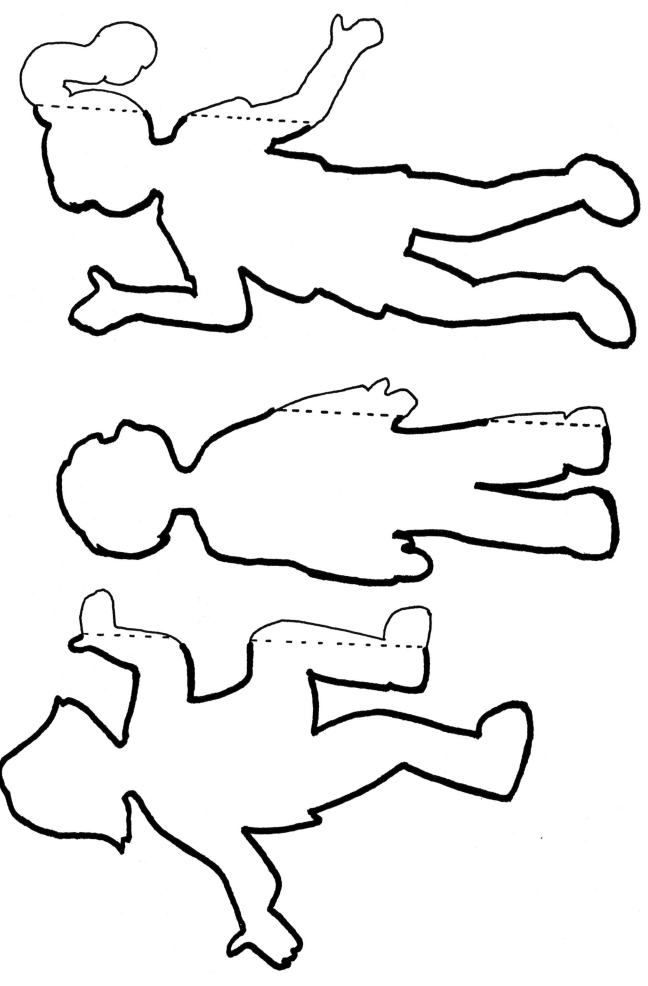

EXTENDING
SHADOWS

MAKE SHADOW PICTURES. Have students search magazines for pictures of people engaged in various activities. Each student should cut the person out of the background, trace the outline of the person's shape onto a sheet of white paper, and then color the shape with a black crayon or marker. The student should paste the picture slightly below and to the side of the "shadow."

SHADOWS TELL ON US. For a variation of Shadow Pictures, follow the same steps as outlined above, omitting the pasting of the picture in front of the "shadow." Let students guess what the person in the original picture is doing by looking at a "shadow picture."

STORY STARTERS
- What would happen if shadows became bored with being "copy-cats" and ran away?
- Write about a shadow that gets lost and can't find his or her "person."
- Write about the day the shadow sees the groundhog.

39

The Queen of Hearts

A VALENTINE'S DAY PAPER CAPER

PREPARATION: Minimal preparation makes a prop that can be used time after time. Follow directions on pages 41 and 42. You will see that you will have a queen with a very long skirt who can become a queen with a Valentine behind her.

(Start story with heart halves pulled down to form a skirt, as shown on page 42.)

THE QUEEN OF HEARTS

The Queen of Hearts
Made some tarts,
All on one Valentine's Day.
The Queen of Hearts
Served those tarts,
And she gave them all away!

None of the tarts are left;
They were so tasty and fine.
So the Queen of Hearts,
Who has no tarts, has sent this Valentine!

(Pull heart halves up behind Queen to form a Valentine.)

Duplicate on red or pink construction paper. Punch out holes where indicated using paper punch. Cut apart the two heart halves.

THE QUEEN OF HEARTS

Reproduce on white paper. Color appropriately and cut out

← Punch out hole on belt using hole punch

Turn two heart halves **BACKWARDS** so that straight edges are on outside

Overlap and match holes

straight side

Overlap Queen of Hearts, Push brad first through "queen" then through heart halves and secure on back.

Down-the heart halves form a skirt, but when pulled up they become a valentine behind the queen.

Push each side up to form a valentine behind queen!

The Queen of Hearts

The "paper caper" provided with this selection would be a great crafts project for students. Teach students the simple verses and duplicate the pages so that they can make "paper caper Valentines" to share at home.

You might also want every student in your classroom to be a "King" or "Queen of Hearts"!

Valentine "crowns" can be worn 2 ways!

Reproduce the pattern on page 44, and give each student two copies. Demonstrate an "accordion fold" for students, showing them how to make sure the dark-line pattern remains on top.

The dotted lines are fold lines. Students should cut only on the dark lines of the pattern. Each student will then need to tape the two strips together, fit to his or her head, trim any excess, and tape the two ends to form the "crown."

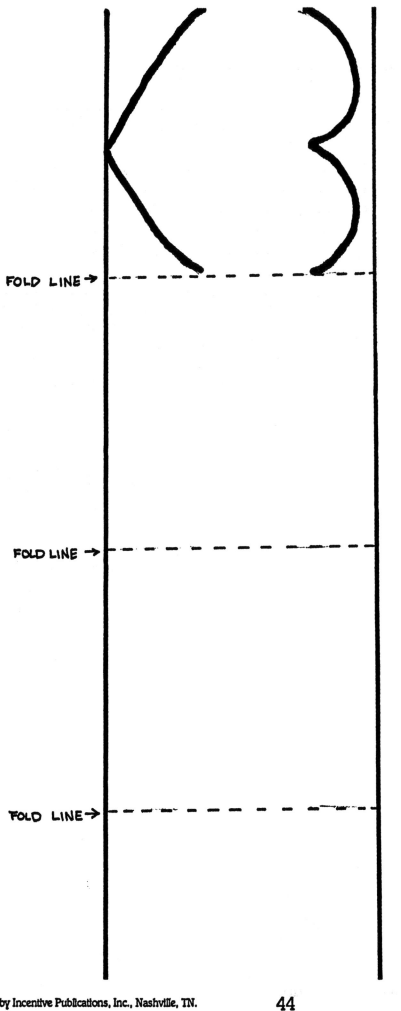

THE KING
AND QUEEN
OF HEARTS
CROWN PATTERN

FOLD LINE →

FOLD LINE →

FOLD LINE →

The Queen of Hearts is
COOKING UP RESEARCH

Use this selection as an opportunity to encourage student research of Valentine's Day. Make ten copies of the tart pattern at the bottom of this page on brown paper. Outline the decoration with squeeze paint in red or pink, or outline in glue and sprinkle with red or pink glitter. Allow to dry thoroughly, and then fold on dotted fold line. Inside each "tart," write one of the research questions given on the following page (be sure to number the questions to make for easier checking). Attach a small magnetic strip to the back of each and attach to a real cookie sheet. Display the cookie sheet along with several books about the holiday and the "V" volume of several sets of encyclopedias. Have the students number sheets to ten and allow them to work in small groups or individually at the center throughout the day. Give all groups or individuals completing (or nearly completing!) the task a real tart at the end of the day.

Using magnetic strips, attach "tarts" to a real cookie sheet!

THE QUEEN OF HEARTS
RESEARCH QUESTIONS AND ANSWERS

QUESTIONS TO RECOPY ON "TARTS":

1. On what date is Valentine's Day celebrated?
2. Who was "Valentine"?
3. When were the first commercial valentines made?
4. What does it mean to "wear your heart on your sleeve"?
5. Who celebrated Lupercalia?
6. Who is Cupid?
7. In what country is it the custom to send pressed snowdrops on Valentine's Day?
8. Who is believed to have sent the first valentine card?
9. During which war did valentines become popular in the United States?

ANSWERS

1. February 14
2. The early Christian church is believed to have had several saints of this name. There are various legends attached: one saint is credited with having healed a young girl of blindness; another is said to have been a great friend to children, but lost his life when he refused to honor Roman gods during the 3rd century A.D.
3. The first commercial valentines were made in the early 1800s.
4. This term means that you make no secret of who your sweetheart is. It supposedly began with a custom developed in the 1700s, according to which groups of young men met to draw young ladies' names and then pinned these to their sleeves.
5. The Romans celebrated Lupercalia. This celebration is thought to be a forerunner of Valentine's Day.
6. Cupid is the Roman god of love, often depicted as a chubby baby with wings bearing a bow and arrows. When his arrow hits a human, the human falls in love!
7. Snowdrops are flowers. They are pressed and sent as greetings in Denmark.
8. The Duke of Orleans, who was imprisoned in the Tower of London in the early 1400s, supposedly sent valentines to his wife in France.
9. The Civil War

BUTTER FLY into SPRING

PREPARATION: There is little to prepare for sharing this simple spring poem. Duplicate the pattern on page 48 using brightly-colored paper. Fold lengthwise along fold line with pattern on outside. Cut out the pattern as you recite. Do not open until the end of the poem.

BUTTER FLY INTO SPRING!

Instruct children that you would like them to recite "butterfly, butterfly, butterfly" as you finish each verse. Practice a few times.

	I feel it, I smell it.
	I know it's somewhere near.
	Butter fly and look!
	Spring is almost here!
(Together)	Butterfly, butterfly, butterfly!
	Butter fly into closets,
	And bring out spring clothes.
	Butter fly out the door,
	And wiggle your toes!
(Together)	Butterfly, butterfly, butterfly!
	Butter fly to the garden,
	And plant a flower or two.
	Butter fly into the yard.
	We've spring pick-up to do.
(Together)	Butterfly, butterfly, butterfly!
	Butter fly away winter!
	Spring's here instead!
	Butter fly to get ready!
	Warm days are ahead!
(Together)	Butterfly, butterfly, butterfly!

Unfold and show audience butterfly.

HOLD IN BACK BY FOLD & "FLUTTER" THE BUTTERFLY!

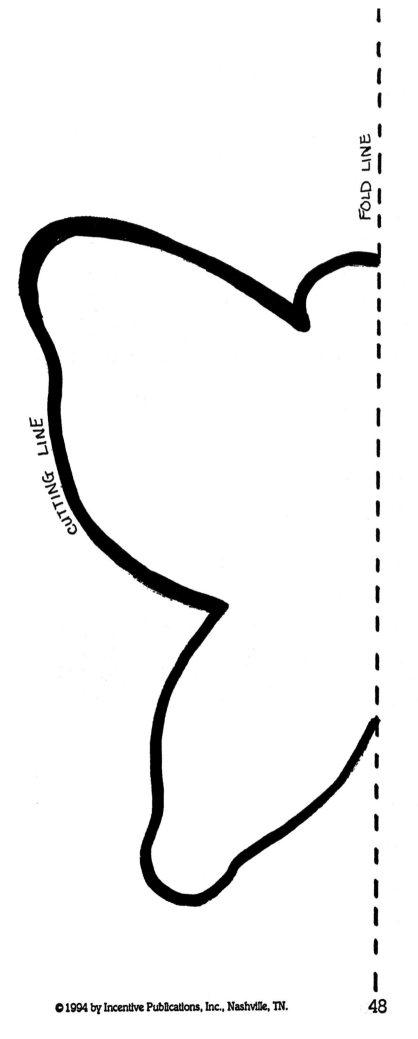

FOLD LINE

CUTTING LINE

WATERCOLOR BUTTERFLIES. Children will "ooh" and "ah" with delight over the beautiful results of this simple "no-fail" art project! Trace the outline of the butterfly pattern on page 50 onto a piece of stiff posterboard and cut out. (If you are dealing with a very large group, make several of these patterns.) Have each student lay the pattern on a piece of black construction paper and trace around it with chalk. Then instruct students to cut out their butterfly shapes, leaving the outsides of the paper intact so that they have butterfly-shaped windows. On a sheet of watercolor paper, each student will paint bands of "spring" colors, letting the colors "bleed," flow, and fade together, with spontaneous results. There should be no attempt at picture-making. When the watercolors are dry, staple or glue the black page with the cut-out space over the watercolor page, and voila—beautiful butterflies!

Hint: when tracing pattern leave off "antennae." This will make cutting easier for little hands!

WRITING. Turn the poem's theme into a "springboard" (pun intended) for students' own creative writing endeavors. Use the "nonthreatening" format provided. Reproduce the pattern on page 50. Instruct students to write after each letter in the word "butterfly" (except the "y," which is already done) a word or phrase about spring that begins with that letter. Here is an example:

B eaming sunshine
U mbrellas sometimes
T ulips springing up
T rees budding
E legant hats on ladies
R obins flying by
F luttering butterflies
L ittle rabbits hopping
Y ou'll love flying

INTO SPRING!

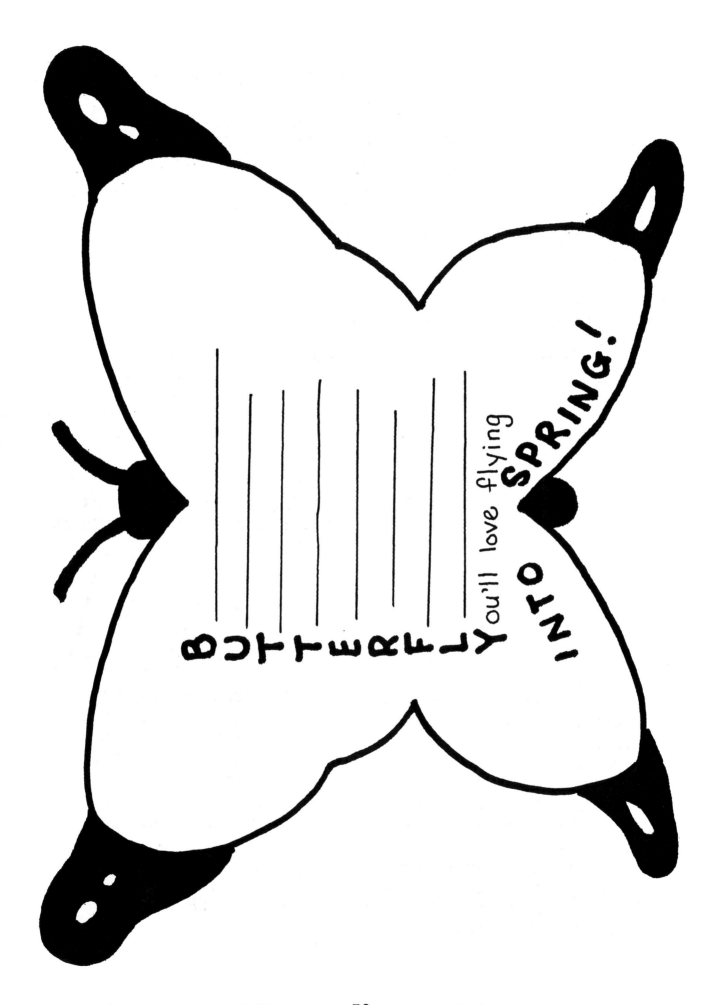

BUTTERFLY You'll love flying INTO SPRING!

SARAH'S PRIZE EGG

AN EASTER EGG SCISSOR-TALE

PREPARATION: Duplicate page 53 on purple paper. Fold in half lengthwise, keeping cutting guide on outside. Fold a sheet of pink paper in half lengthwise and keep near you as you tell the story.

purple   pink

SARAH'S PRIZE EGG

Sarah was up bright and early on Easter morning. She could hardly control her excitement as she scrambled to pull on her clothes and tie her shoes. Easter eggs would be hidden in her yard, and she was anxious to find a very special one. She had asked that the prize egg be in her very favorite colors: purple and pink! This was the egg she wanted to find first of all!

Sarah bounced outside and began to search for her special prize egg. She made a broad path through the front yard *(cut out section A on purple paper)*. No egg!

She made a broad path through the back yard *(cut out section B)*. No egg!

She zig-zagged all around the house *(cut out section C as you talk)*, peering very carefully behind all the trees and all the bushes. She found a few eggs, but not the prize egg!

Sarah was disappointed. "Maybe," she thought, "I'm just not looking hard enough in all the little places." So she peeked in all the little hidey-holes she could think of *(use paper punch to cut holes in area D)*. Still no prize egg!

"Well," thought Sarah, "I'm going to look in one more little place." *(Cut out section E.)* So she did, and this is what she found!

(Slide folded pink paper inside folded purple paper. Open the two sheets together to reveal Sarah's prize egg.)

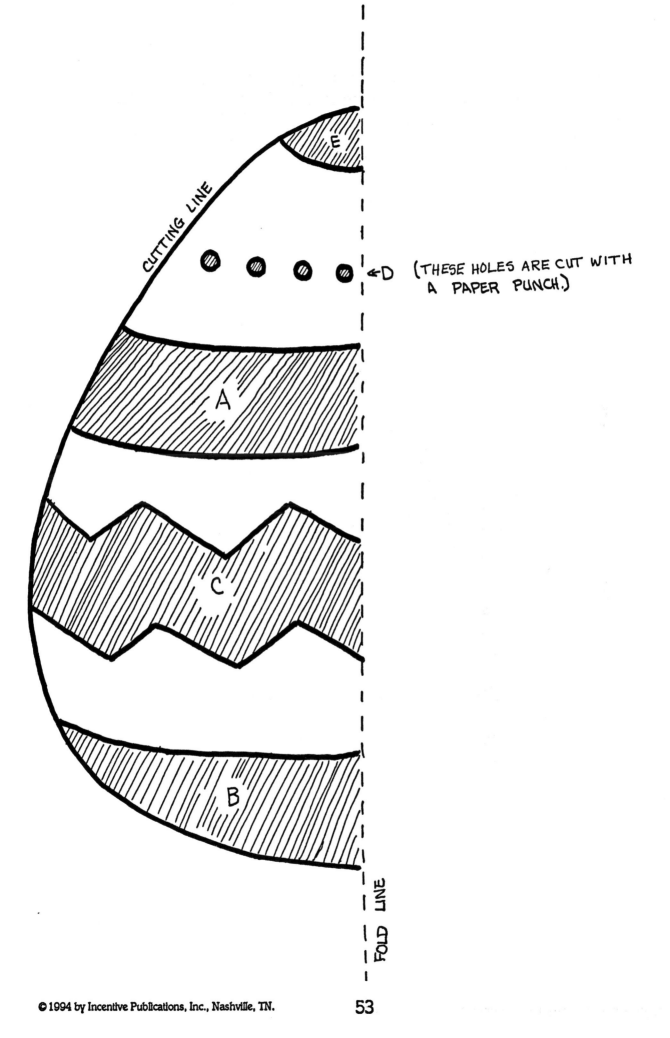

CUTTING LINE

←D (THESE HOLES ARE CUT WITH A PAPER PUNCH.)

E

A

C

B

FOLD LINE

SARAH'S Prize egg

Do some "egg-citing" activities as a follow-up to "Sarah's Prize Egg." Have students create their own prize eggs using favorite colors. Instruct them to:

① Fold a sheet of construction paper lengthwise.

② Draw ½ an egg shape on the fold.

③ They may then make an even number of lines (curving, straight, zig-zagging, etc.)

In order for the egg to assume an egg shape, there needs to be an even number of lines, and students must cut out the top and bottom and all alternate sections in-between. Slide another favorite color behind the page to create a prize egg.

Have each student create a personalized prize egg using the pattern shown. Note that the name should completely fill egg shape. Choose two colored markers, and fill in letters with one color and background with another.

EGG-SPRESSIONS. Have students figure out the "egg-spressions" on page 55. Copy the "Red Riding Hood's Basket" pattern found on page 56. Students then cut out eggs and write the meanings of the expressions on the eggs' backs. Give each student a basket pattern and let students glue their eggs to it, putting all their eggs in one basket.

EGG-spressions

What do these expressions mean? Cut out the eggs and write your answers on their backs (or underneath the questions). Glue the eggs to the basket pattern your teacher provides and "put all your eggs in one basket"!

WHAT DOES IT MEAN TO...

(If you have written the answers to the questions on the backs of the eggs, simply attach each egg to the basket with a single dab of glue.)

to put all your eggs in one basket?

to get your nest made?

to be a rotten egg?

to be a good egg?

to be an egghead?

to walk on egg shells?

to have egg on your face?

to count your chicks before they hatch?

to shell out?

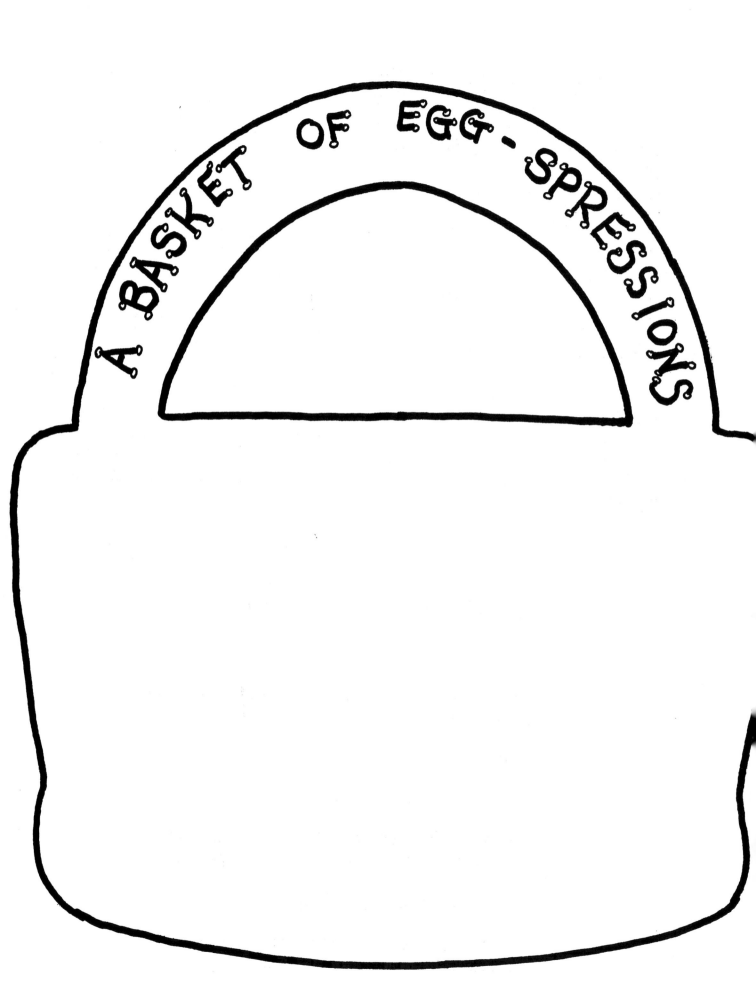

A BASKET OF EGG-SPRESSIONS

56

MOTHER'S DAY IS COMING!

PREPARATION: Using markers, color with appropriate colors the items in the gift shape on page 59. Cut out shape. Color the gift on page 60 or duplicate it on a single sheet of brightly-colored paper. Cut out and glue to matching shape, gluing blank sides together. As you tell the story, hold the outside of the gift toward audience and the side with items toward yourself.

MOTHER'S DAY IS COMING!

I haven't any money; it's sad, but it's true.
Mother's Day is coming. What am I to do?

(Hold up "gift.")

If I can't buy a gift, I can do something else instead.
I know! I'll bring Mom breakfast in bed!

(For Father's Day, substitute "Dad.")

(Begin cutting out "toast.")

Of course, I'm not big enough to cook—just almost,
But I'm sure Mom would enjoy jam on a piece of toast.

(Begin cutting out "dish.")

And on Mother's Day, I'm sure Mom would wish
That she needn't wash a single dish!

(Begin cutting out "garbage can.")

Carry out the garbage; that's something I can do.
That wouldn't be too hard, and it's quite useful, too!

(Begin cutting out "broom.")

I'm very handy with dustcloth and broom;
Mom would be pleased if I cleaned my room.

(Begin cutting out "flower.")

Mom loves flowers of every color and hue,
And I know where to find one that's a beautiful bright blue.

(For Father's Day, substitute: "Not just moms love flowers;
dads love them, too!")

(Begin cutting out "heart.")

A few minutes ago I didn't know where to start,
And now I know I can give the love that's in my heart!

DISCARD BLACK AREAS AS YOU SNIP ITEMS FROM PACKAGE

COLOR ITEMS APPROPRIATELY BEFORE TELLING STORY.

* NOTE: FOR FATHER'S DAY, SIMPLY "WHITE OUT" THE WORD "MOM" AND WRITE "DAD."

Cut out around outside edges.

HAPPY MOTHER'S DAY, MOM!

Color appropriate colors or duplicate on a single sheet of brightly—colored paper. Glue to back of page 59 after cutting out.

* Note: For Father's Day simply "white out" message on tag and print Happy Father's Day, Dad!

Extending the Poem — MOTHER'S DAY IS COMING!

Turn this "paper caper" into a gift for Mom. Reproduce and distribute the gift pattern on page 60. On the back of his or her gift, each student will write a special promise—something he or she will do for Mom on Mother's Day.

Mom, I promise to dust and run the vacuum for you!

Or simply use the gift pattern to make a Mother's Day card. On the back, each student will use a marker to write:

M
O
T
H
E
R

YOU'RE THE WHOLE PACKAGE!

Using each letter (and a writing instrument of a different color), have each student write a word or phrase about his or her mother.

Mom
c**O**oks favorite things
and always **T**ucks me in!
She **H**ugs me
Everyday!
I **R**eally love her!

You're the whole package! Love, Jan

I KNOW A SECRET!

A Birthday Paper Caper

Use this "paper caper" to announce the birthday of a child in your classroom or group and, at the same time, to reinforce the importance of following instructions!

PREPARATION: Duplicate page 64 on brightly-colored paper. Fold along fold line so that pattern and message appear on the outside. Now follow preparation instructions below.

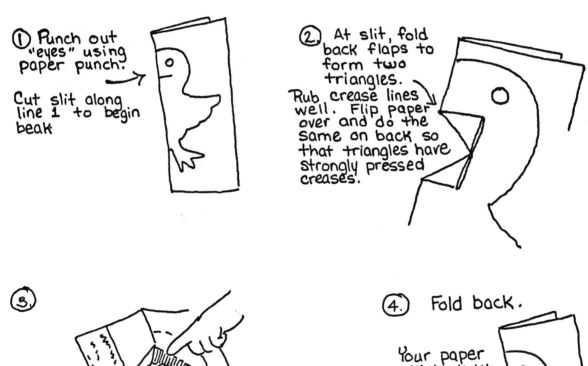

① Punch out "eyes" using paper punch!

Cut slit along line 1 to begin beak

② At slit, fold back flaps to form two triangles. Rub crease lines well. Flip paper over and do the same on back so that triangles have strongly pressed creases.

③.

Now open the paper up, and push the triangles through to the other side of the paper!

④ Fold back.

Your paper will look like this - but when you open it up, you will see that you have two eyes and a "beak" that looks like it is "talking" as you open and close the paper!

I KNOW A SECRET!

Announce to the class that you received a strange message in your mailbox today. Hold up the folded paper. *(Be sure the pattern is on the side you hold toward yourself.)*

Point out that in the corner is a message that reads, "To learn a secret, follow these instructions!" Cut off the instructions and hand them to a student, asking him or her to read the instructions aloud, one at a time, so that you can follow them.

As the instructions are read, use your cutting lines on the opposite side of the pattern to do exactly what is said. For example, when the child reads, "Number One: Make three zig-zags," you will be cutting out the feet.

When instructions are finished, open up the pattern to reveal a "bird with a talking beak" in your hands, and announce, "Today is _____'s birthday! Do you want to know how I know? I know because a little bird told me so."

If you wish, you
can write a "birthday
message" inside
so that it will appear on
the "little bird" after you
have cut him out.

Give the "little bird"
to the birthday child!

TO LEARN A SECRET, FOLLOW THESE
INSTRUCTIONS!

1. Make three zig-zags.
2. Make a middle-sized curve.
3. Make three ocean waves.
4. Make a dip to the left.
5. SMILE BIG BECAUSE NOW I'M
   GOING TO TELL YOU MY SECRET!

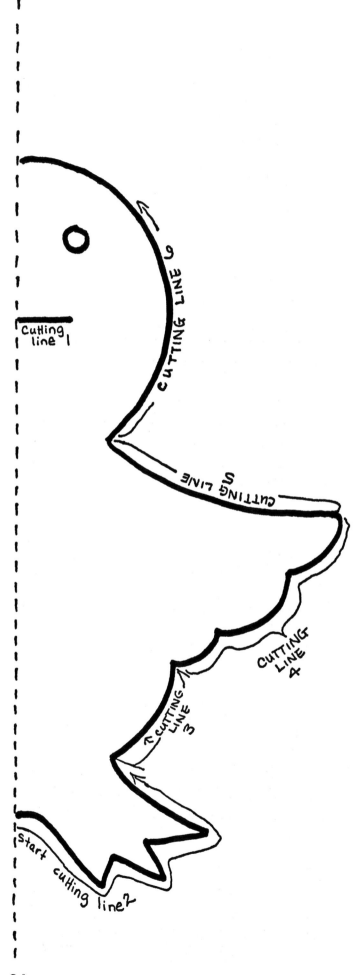

Cutting
line 1

CUTTING LINE 6

CUTTING LINE 5

CUTTING
LINE 4

CUTTING
LINE 3

Start cutting line 2

I HAVE A SECRET!

Use a birthday as an opportunity to make a student feel extra special for a day. Here's a unique idea to do just that.

THE BIRTHDAY CHILD TAKES THE CAKE. Create a winning display in your classroom that can be used all year long to give a birthday child a special treat from you! Reproduce the sign on page 66. Color with bright markers and then laminate. You can use dry markers to write the child's name on the blank line and later wipe it off with a damp cloth to make it ready to use again. Reproduce a quantity of the "cupcakes" shown below on various colors of paper. Label each with a variety of teacher treats: homework pass, extra five minutes recess, extra five points in any subject, extra recreational reading time, etc. Display "cupcakes" in a real muffin tin, as shown, with the sign posted above.

Today is your BIRTHDAY, HEATHER! so you take the cake!

The birthday child may go to the display and take the cake, choosing any privilege he or she would like!
(Note: Don't leave out children with summer birthdays. Give them each a day of their own during the last month of school.)

HOMEWORK PASS   10 MIN. "FREE TIME"

LINE LEADER

Today is your **BIRTHDAY**! So take the **CAKE**! of you

The PAPER CAPER PEOPLE

Let the "Paper Caper People" make holidays special in your school! Most of the stories in *Scissor-Tales for Special Days* are geared toward a primary audience, but you will find even intermediate students enthralled with the "paper magic" and interested when you ask them to become "Paper Caper People" and entertain primary classrooms over the holidays throughout the school year! Teachers have long been aware of the bonuses of sharing the skills of older students with the younger ones. Using the Paper Caper Storytelling Program has many benefits:

- Speaking and presenting experience for intermediate students
- Experience following directions to achieve desired outcomes for intermediate students
- Literature and learning tie-ins for classrooms
- Enjoyment for primary groups
  And. . .
- Great public relations for your classroom!

HERE'S HOW TO BEGIN:

1. Introduce to your intermediate students some scissor-tales, explaining that you would like to set up appointments with primary groups at holiday times throughout the year for these to be shared. They are invited to become "Paper Caper People" and do the sharing!

2. Duplicate enough copies of different stories so that each student may have one. It is fine if more than one student has the same story, because they can present to different classrooms. (Hint: It is a good idea to duplicate several copies of the paper caper portion of the stories so that students can practice.) As each holiday season approaches, give the "Paper Caper People" for that particular season copies of their stories.

3. If you do not have time for practice in the classroom, put the students in pairs or groups to practice during free time, and allow them to take their selections home to work with their families and friends. Use this as a creative homework assignment! Some of the selections require paper capers that are prepared ahead of time and can be used again and again. These need be "worked" only during the story. These can be made at home or during an art lesson at school.

4. Have a follow-up day on which students present their stories to each other and to you!

5. Announce your program to primary classrooms by sending them the announcement on page 70. Post a sign-up sheet in the teachers' lounge listing dates and times students can present. Teachers interested in the program can sign up for a visit from your students.

6. Send to each interested classroom a confirmation card (page 71). Ideas and patterns on page 72 make the card adaptable to any holiday season. You may also choose to duplicate the extension page for the story to be presented and staple it to the confirmation card. The classroom teacher may wish to carry out one of the suggested activities as a follow-up.

7. Post a schedule in your classroom and inform your students of the dates and times of their presentations.

8. Give each of the "Paper Caper People" an award (page 73). (Hint: You might also want to videotape some of the storytellers as they perform to show to interested storytellers another year.)

now booking appearances...
The
PAPER CAPER PEOPLE

The "Paper Caper People" in _____'s room want to celebrate the holiday with primary classrooms. They have learned some very special stories using paper techniques. A sign-up sheet, listing dates and times available is located _____. If you would like the "Paper Caper People" to visit *your classroom*, please schedule there!

Hope to see you Soon!

Confirmation Card

There's no better way to confirm a visit from the "Paper Caper People" than <u>with</u> a paper caper! This card is a "pop-up" adaptable to <u>each</u> holiday!

① Fold a sheet of paper in half.

② On the folded edge, fold the top left corner down to form a triangle.

③ Unfold the triangle & open the card. Pull the triangle to the inside of the card.

Closed, it looks like this.

④ Duplicate the illustration appropriate to the holiday from the following page. Trim along outside edges and fold in half. Then glue to the triangle on your card so that the top sticks up.

Choose the appropriate slogan from below to write on your card or make up your own. Add the date, time, storyteller, and title of the story to be shared.

Halloween: The Paper Caper Storytellers are looking forward to a BOO-TIFUL time with your class!

Thanksgiving: The Paper Caper Storytellers will be visiting your class. We'll have GOBBLES of fun!

Christmas: HO, HO, HO, lots of good fun in store!

Valentine's Day: The Paper Caper People can HEARTLY wait!

Easter: HOPPING to see you soon!

72

Thanks,

for being one of the

PAPER CAPER PEOPLE

and telling a good holiday story with all the "trimmings"!

_____
Teacher

_____
Date

PAPER CAPER BOOKMARKS
(make up your <u>own</u> story!)

Use scissor-tales to motivate writing experiences. Use these bookmarks as idea starters!

Making up your own scissor-tales need not be complicated. The bookmarks on the next few pages provide good starting places. Each bookmark should be creased along its dotted fold line. A student should count to see how many cuts would be needed to smoothly trim the image from the paper. Now the student can take any of several different approaches to building a story around the cutting of the bookmark, always keeping the final outcome in mind.

- Each cut can symbolize something: character name, "went in," "around here," behind there," etc.
- A student might write a poem or story, making a cut after each verse or portion.

Here are the patterns, and the wonderful imaginations of children can supply the stories! Encourage them to create their own patterns, too, when they feel ready.

AUTUMN LEAF

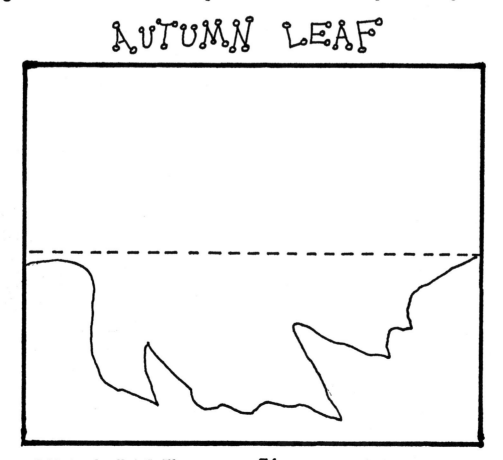

WITCH

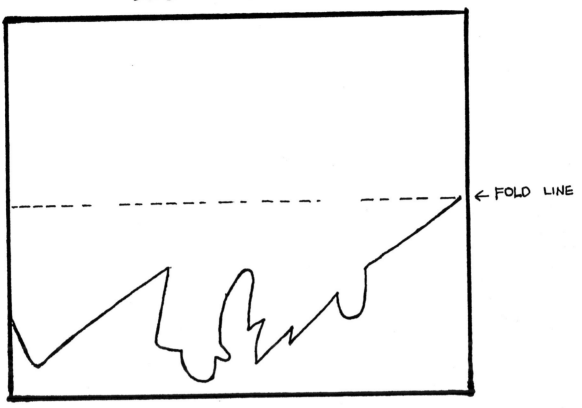

← FOLD LINE

RABBIT

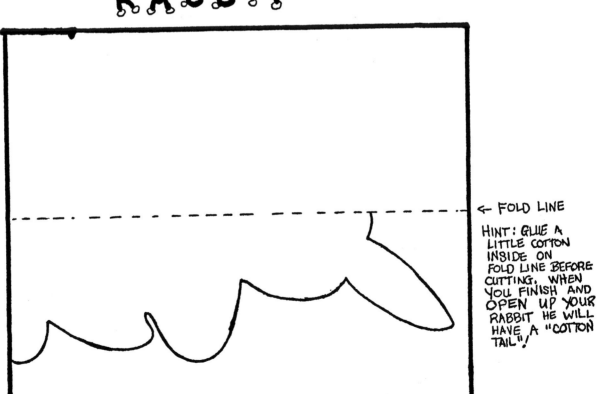

← FOLD LINE

HINT: GLUE A LITTLE COTTON INSIDE ON FOLD LINE BEFORE CUTTING. WHEN YOU FINISH AND OPEN UP YOUR RABBIT HE WILL HAVE A "COTTON TAIL"!

SNOWMAN

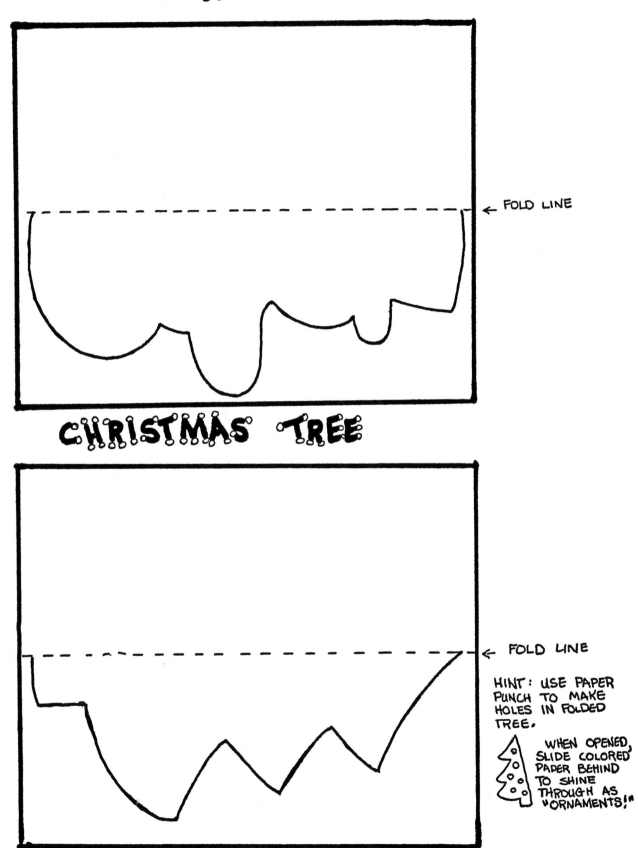

← FOLD LINE

CHRISTMAS TREE

← FOLD LINE

HINT: USE PAPER PUNCH TO MAKE HOLES IN FOLDED TREE.

WHEN OPENED, SLIDE COLORED PAPER BEHIND TO SHINE THROUGH AS "ORNAMENTS!"

SHAMROCK

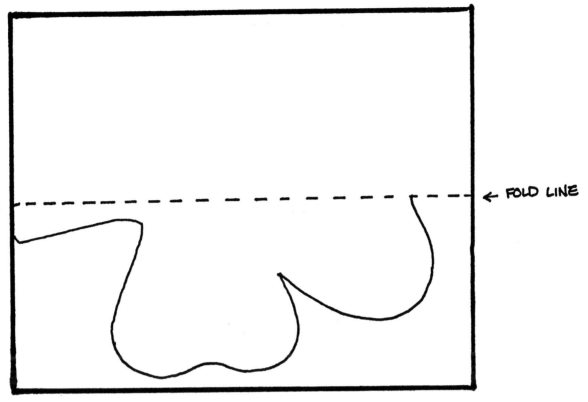

← FOLD LINE

SCARECROW

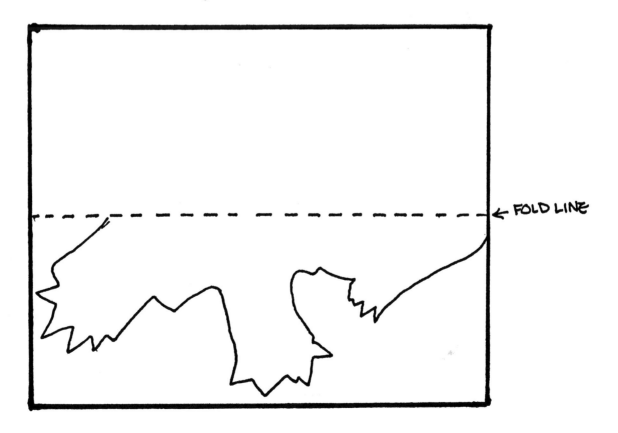

← FOLD LINE

BIRTHDAY OR CLOWN HAT

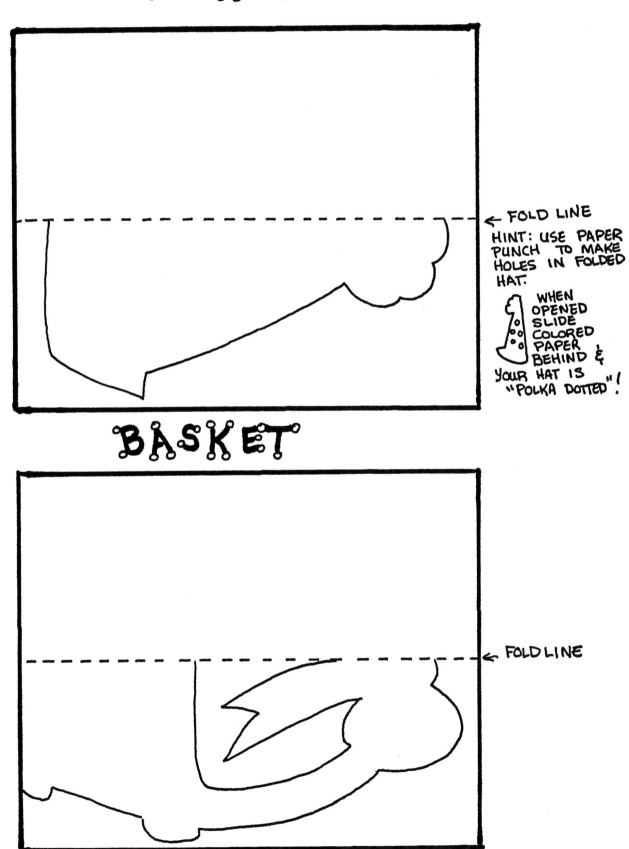

← FOLD LINE

HINT: USE PAPER PUNCH TO MAKE HOLES IN FOLDED HAT.

WHEN OPENED SLIDE COLORED PAPER BEHIND & YOUR HAT IS "POLKA DOTTED"!

BASKET

← FOLD LINE